Whoever's reading this you will feel a sense of sadness. You may begin to relive some things from your past that you tried to forget. You may laugh and you may also cry. Most importantly you will relate to most of the pieces I have so carefully chosen to put into this book. My goal is not for you to be entertained, but for you to reach deep inside yourself. My goal is for you to be able to look every detrimental situation in the face and not feel ashamed. The things you have gone through taught you something valuable. If you are still experiencing these things maybe you haven't been able to see the lesson yet. After reading this I hope you realize the person that you were does not define you. The pain you feel or have felt was only temporary. The tears you cry are just a result of a breakthrough waiting to happen. Also you can't love whole heartedly until you first love the person you see in the mirror daily. I am not perfect I am still learning as well. I hope you take something good away from me and forgive

me as I fall. I am still a work in progress myself. I am

simply a woman who has been through experiences that

have been bad but made me better. Ladies I promise that we

are more alike than what we think. While it is okay to be

vulnerable, we must take everything we go through and

learn from it. Whoever's reading this, I am Aliyah Michelle

and this is S.H.E.

I was taught to never question God, but I always wondered why he couldn't let you stay here a little longer. Thoughts of you fill my mind daily. I can't help but feel like a piece of me is gone forever. What keeps me going is the solace of believing that you are somewhere smiling. I know you are somewhere laughing even though I can't hear it. You are somewhere much happier than you were here on earth. In my heart is where I will forever keep the memories, lessons and the experiences we shared. I love you and miss you so much. I wish you were here. This is for you Dad.

Suffer (/ˈsəfər/):

To undergo or feel pain or distress.

You never really get over the death of a

loved one. You just learn to suppress the pain

well enough to be able to move on with life.

-Aliyah Michelle

I Cried For You

So I cried for you last night

I hate to be emotional but I thought about you all night long

I curled up in a ball, the tears began to fall

and I cried for you

The anniversary of your death is approaching

All month long I've been praying and hoping for the

strength to get by just like any other day

But that day constantly replays

No pause or fast forward so with all the strength I have I go

towards it

Until the day comes and I break down

January is a month that I hate now

All the holidays and birthdays you can't make now

And the way that I'm feeling I can't shake now

And I know I'm being selfish so I apologize to you

I wanna see your face but reminiscing is all that I can do

Trying to smile with how I'm feeling right now seems so

impossible

I just wanna hold your hand I wanna follow you

I want you to hold me, wipe my tears and do the things that

fathers do

But that will never happen please tell me what am I to do?

I had a dream we were in heaven I was standing right

beside of you

Then I woke up and didn't see you

That's when I cried for you

Strong Friend

I know we all have our own lives

And so often we forget to take a little time

To make that phone call or send that text

To that friend we haven't seen in a while

And sometimes life has so many ups and downs

And our loved ones don't know this

There were times where I felt like I was drowning and

nobody noticed

And nobody was calling, and I barely got a message

I had so many demons and nobody was checking

to see if I was ok

Sometimes silence is our worst enemy and our biggest

demon can be assumption

Feeling like we have all the time in the world so when we

go days without speaking it's nothing

Mentally and physically their in pain and never say so

Sadly sometimes people don't want to wait until the storm

ends to see if it's gonna be a rainbow

Check on your friends

Especially that strong one that says everything is fine

Fighting battles by themselves with tears in their eyes

Find out whats wrong and if you can help them get by

You just might end up doing what they need to stay alive

Everybody Black

Is it protect and serve? Or suspect and hurt or kill them
dead?

What's the procedure when a cop has a gun to your head?

Somebody asked me what would I do if that was my son

I ain't a killer but these days I've been thinking like one

All black, one mask, just me and my gun

Y'all wanna live by that shit then y'all will die by one

Y'all think its sweet?

I ain't going out here screaming no justice no peace

How about no justice for the cop who would take
somebody from me

Y'all think its fair to use your power to kill these kids dead
in the street

then get put on administrative leave?

So y'all got paid for that?

Out here still collecting a check while the parents still feel
the pain from that

And I can't even blame the cops because I checked the
numbers

More than half of the brothers that were killed over the
summer

Were by the hands of another brother

We are killing each other

This world ain't nice

I pray and speak life into all the black people before I sleep

at night

I'm trying to stay positive but as quiet as it's kept

The only thing I keep thinking in my head is who's next?

Listen to your heart. Especially when it's
crying.
-Aliyah Michelle

Love Song

As I lay in bed on a tear stained pillow case

I feel your face creep in between my thighs

I close my eyes as you lay sweet kisses on my other lips

As you prepare to drink from my fountain

I'm not doubting that the moment won't be pleasurable

But how is this supposed to make up

For the fact that in the morning I have to pat my face with

makeup

There's not enough concealer to conceal the wrath of your

anger

In your arms is where I'm supposed to feel safe

But when you lift your hands to me it isn't for an embrace,

but a sign of danger

What did I do to make you mad this time?

For I have been your maid, your sex slave, and everything

else you deem necessary

But what's necessary for me I have yet to receive

You tell me you love me but your words fall on deaf ears

same song different tune

Praying that one day you will at least switch the melody

because love isn't supposed to hurt

All you do is cry, and tell the same lie about how there

won't be a next time

But the next time is even worse than the previous

I'm kneeling down crying out God are you seeing this?

Every day this man beats me senseless and annihilates my

existence and

You've granted me not even the slightest bit of mercy

God take me into your arms so he can no longer hurt me

They say you give your toughest battles to your strongest

soldiers but I have reached my breaking point

I wave the white flag no longer caring to be the victor

I am the victim but he constantly depicts me as the villain

I just want my peace, I just want my zen again,

but it's so far from my mental

It's like trying to touch a star with my index finger or my

middle while my feet are still planted on the ground

It's not that simple

God gave me a mouth to speak and hands to fight and feet

to move

Why is it that I can't walk away from you?

Is it because I'm trapped in this toxic cycle?

Or fear of meeting another mother fucker just like you?

And you say I'll never find someone who treats me

like you do

If only I can get that in writing

Signed sealed and delivered so I will never fall into the

hands of another tyrant

You oppressively use your power never seeing your faults

or admitting your wrongs

I finally realized who you were all along

I've grown so weary of your love and I'm tired of your

song

I've finally found the strength to move on

I'm so far gone

Invisible

You acknowledge my reaction

But not what you did to make it happen

Feelings of anger sadness and defeat over come me

You push the knife in deeper then where the last man left it

And then you blame me when it bleeds

The sound of your voice is violent

Forcing me to stay silent

Tears roll down my cheeks and you pretend not to see

I don't know this individual

This pain is unforgettable

I hate you and I hate myself

I wish I was invisible

Single Mother

I never asked to be another statistic

Just another woman raising a kid all by herself

Working two jobs getting no sleep to make ends meet

And the daddy don't give no help

But I don't complain, because I already know what people

are going to say

"Well, you knew exactly how that nigga was and you had a

baby by him anyway?"

But who is anybody to judge?

No relationship is all kisses and hugs and shit like that

And do you really think I had any type of clue that he

would treat my kid like that?

A father and son bond is supposed to be sacred and time is

something you don't get back

A few minutes out of your day just to talk to him or play

and my baby can't even get that

So to whom this may concern

I am not an angry black woman

I am not a bitter baby mother looking for a come up

When I don't have it I work or come up with a way to get it

Because no matter how much I stress his needs to his daddy

his selfish ass just don't listen

You were raised by a single woman

yet you choose to defame me so much

The irony,

Growing up to be just like that absentee father you swear

you hated so much

Do you know what it's like to go to school for five hours,

see your child for two

Then go to work until the next day? I do

And when he's sick and he needs comfort and love from his

parent

Who takes off work to give him that? Not you

There were times when I used to feel so bad

I wanted him to be close with you like I was with my dad

But you can't force a man to do anything

That's something I had to figure out

At the end of the day, my son is ok

He's the one who's really missing out

And no I can't teach him how to be a man but I'll make

sure he don't continue that cycle

And I don't care if my baby is a splitting image of you I

promise he'll be nothing like you

He'll have everything he needs as long as my heart beats

I don't care what you do on social media and what you tell

people in the streets

It stopped being about us a long time ago

The minute that little boy was conceived

I started making plans for his life

before he even had the chance to breathe

So to whom this may concern

I'm not angry I'm not bitter

I'm just over it and done

And I swear that I don't even hate his father

I just really love my son

I'm going to do my best to raise him

I'm going to love him like no other

This is the story of my life and others

Sincerely, A single mother

At times we are so afraid to start over that we will adjust to what's hurting us instead of moving on. Situations don't always get better, sometimes you just get used to it. But no one should ever grow accustomed to pain.

-Aliyah Michelle

Stupid

So I guess I'm just your stupid bitch?

Your play thing?

Your something to do when its nothing to do

And my feelings mean nothing to you

That call at 3 in the morning

That "I miss you" text when she's gotten on your nerves

And I know sooner or later your going to try to

make things work

But you're mine for the evening

She still needs some time

so now you're mine for the weekend

There I am making your favorite dish and washing the

dishes

In the bedroom doing all kinds of positions

Moving my tongue with precision

Pleasing you is my mission and at that I never fail

You said I was your little secret so I'll never tell

Even though I want to so bad

I swear you and I could be great

All this hiding I hate

I know that it's wrong

But I don't want to be right if it's going to send you away

I constantly fight myself

like girl he's taken don't get too pressed

When you leave me its like I lose my breath

Then you and her are right back like y'all never left

And I'm left alone

At home sipping jack and coke like it's going out of style

Acting like I ain't tripping putting on a fake smile

Meanwhile making yet another call

when you ignored the first three

Pouring my heart out in text messages you never read

I guess I gotta face it you and I will never be

So I spend the next few days realizing my wrongs

Listening to empowerment songs

Trying to find the strength to put on my big girl thongs

and move on

I won't settle for less than what I deserve

I'm doing my best to realize my worth

I've learned my lesson, I'm done stressing

No longer will I block my blessings

Swearing to all my girlfriends that I'm done

messing with you

Then I finally get a message from you

It was all useless. I'm just stupid.

My Drug

I wish there was something I could take to forget you

Some place I could go to get my mind off of you

Unfortunately for love there is no rehab

And even if there were I'd probably relapse

All pride out the window I'm not afraid to admit that

Your kisses put me at a place of ease

You wouldn't believe how much I think of you when you

aren't here

When you're near I just can't resist your touch

I disappear from the world for days with you

Just once isn't enough

This fix I need for life

I go through withdrawal when I can't get to you

I start having flashbacks whenever someone mentions you

And so many times I swore I was done

Then I'm calling you repeatedly asking for some

There isn't an intervention that can help me end this

I'm in this until I'm finished

Having you in my life is a must

I swear you are like my drug.

No matter how good you are to other people it may never be reciprocated. I make myself available to other people all the time, especially to the men I've had relationships with. You know those people who will give you the shirt off their back even if they are freezing? The people who will give you their last even if they will be broke? The people who will share their favorite food with you even if they are starving? That person was and still is me in some cases. I hate being cold and Lord knows I hate to share my food but If someone I love needs it they can have it. Reality set in when I wasn't getting that same type of love back. People who I thought loved me watched me go without and didn't even think to help. I couldn't fathom how or why people could do something like that to people they claim to care about. Sometimes it takes for you to be in the worst place of your life to see who really has your back. The sad thing is even though that I still feel compelled to help them anyway. This heart of mine is so big I love it and hate it at the same time. However, even unconditional love has to come with conditions too. I'm not ashamed to say I'm still learning that.

These days I'm a lot more focused on staying

true to myself. I often put the wants and needs

of others before my own. What I want should

always be relevant. How I feel should always

matter. I come first and I have to remember

that. -Aliyah Michelle

Mexico

Me and my step dad used to play this game

I'm sure you probably know it,

It goes "Shame shame shame

I don't want to go to Mexico no more more more

There's a big fat policeman at the door door door

If he grabs you by the collar, girl you better holler

I don't wanna go to Mexico no more more more

Shut the door!"

We would play from sun up to sun down

From the time he got home from work

until it was time for bed

We would play that game until I fell asleep

We didn't really care what my momma said

And one day he came home from work

and covered my eyes

Walked me upstairs and said he had a big surprise

Told me baby girl let's go pack your bags

We're going to Mexico for real this time!

I ran upstairs looking for my suitcase and couldn't find it

And little did I know Mexico was in my bedroom closet

He slammed the door behind him

and made sure he locked it

He's touching me and grabbing me

and I'm begging him to stop it

I'm trying my best to holler but he's got me by my collar

Can't breathe, can't scream just crying in despair

We went to Mexico almost everyday until about my

thirteenth year

I wanted to tell my momma sooner

my heart was in so much pain

But all I could feel was shame shame shame

One day I got the courage and I went to her crying

She told me to stay silent

Because she didn't want no policeman at her door door

door

Had the nerve to ask me what did he do that for

What did I say to him and what did I have on

I was 9

Blue shirt, khaki skirt and socks up to my thighs

But I guess it was my fault

I didn't know he was into the school girl look

I didn't know playing a simple game would

cost me my innocence

How could she not believe me?

What kind of thing was that to say?

You question my outfit like that's really the problem

No grown man should ever look at a child that way

Now I'm wishing that I never said anything at all

Nobody to talk to nobody to call

Asking me what's wrong as if she didn't already know

Pain that took years to create and she says

I should let it go

I have nightmares about that closet

I begged that man to let me go

I wish that I was dead and buried

anywhere but Mexico

I don't wanna go to Mexico no more more more

PLEASE! Don't shut the door

Some of the men I've dated had me believing that loving someone meant staying with them even if they hurt you. No matter how much the pain bothered me I was supposed to stay. I guess it doesn't take a rocket scientist to figure out that that's exactly what I did. They cheated and I stayed. They lied and I believed them. Even when I got that little feeling in my gut that it might be a lie I ignored it. I completely went against everything I grew up believing about love. If you know me then you know I am obsessed with movies. My favorites are the ones with a great love story. While I know everything wasn't going to be peaches and cream I'd be damned if my sweet kisses wouldn't turn him into my charming prince. Silly me they did the exact opposite. Maybe I'm not as good at kissing as I thought I was. I have a habit of attracting broken men. For whatever reason I just swear I have what it takes to save them so in most cases the roles are reversed. They are the damsel in distress and I am the one who comes to save them. Sadly I am not rewarded with the upmost respect and love. I wonder did it ever cross their minds that I also might need saving? My past is the farthest thing from pretty but flaws and all I still love like I've never been hurt. Is it too far fetch to want someone who loves like me? I am a hopeless romantic and my dad ain't raise no punk. Giving up on real love isn't an option. As patient as I am I just hope the man of my dreams comes and sweeps me off my feet soon. I am strong but I am tired.

When things in life get rough the hardest
decision is whether to try harder or give up.
And I don't know how to give up yet.
-Aliyah Michelle

At 20 years old I was at an all time low in my life. My father passed away and later that year my best friend went to jail. Shortly after I got evicted from the apartment we shared. Nothing was going how I expected for it to go in my head. After two years of being sick my dad was supposed to make this miraculous recovery. My best friend should have been ruled not guilty on all charges. The opposite of everything I had been praying for happened. I would smile or keep a plain face while in front of family and friends but my heart was in pain. I cried myself to sleep so many nights that year I can't even count. I was so sad and things had gotten bad one night. I couldn't stop myself from crying and I could not go to sleep. I did what I normally would do which was write. What would usually be a poem ended up being my own funeral plans along with a letter to my loved ones. I fell asleep that night and when I woke up in the morning I looked over what I had written and thought about it for hours. I didn't write a will because I didn't have shit to give anyone. I didn't have children so I couldn't leave a legacy. If I died that day what would I be remembered for? Who was going to carry on the memory of my life? I spent years searching for a reason to stay here.

Some time later I fell in what I thought was love. That situation turned out to be one of the biggest lessons of my life. It was also one of my biggest blessings because from that situation came my son. I began writing more and searching for what it was that truly made me happy.

Looking back on that moment I'm so happy I made the decision to live. I now feel like I have a purpose here and I am living it to it's fullest potential. For those who are living in their darkest moments I pray you find your reason for living. It isn't easy at all. It may be an everyday struggle to some. To those who may not understand what this feels like please remember there is always someone who is fighting a battle you don't know anything about. They need

encouragement not your judgement. Be kind.

Go

I wanted to leave

I didn't have anything left in me

Didn't care what people expected of me

Or what they would say

I secluded myself and neglected my needs

And all my responsibilities

I didn't care about my appearance

Or what people thought about me

I wrote an apology to my family

Telling them to forgive me please

But I couldn't help feeling like I wanted to leave

I wanted my heart to stop hurting

I attracted sadness like honey to bees

Like dogs to fleas

Like beauty to the beast

I almost gave in to the feeling of defeat

And I didn't care

But something told me that I'm supposed to be here

So I climbed out of that ditch of doubt

Started to think of everything I bitch about

And I cried

I can't believe what I was willing to leave behind

And it's so hard for me to hide my pain in plain sight

But it's me versus myself and I'm choosing to fight

Racing through the tunnel feels like I'm chasing the light

Finding every reason not to give up on life and go

Death is certain that's something I know

And there are still sometimes where I just feel low

I am here for a reason that's what I believe

I have to keep going.

It's not my time to leave

Them: You can't save everybody

Me: Somebody has to try.

-Aliyah Michelle

You Need You

How many times have you cried after telling the world
you're fine?
How many "I'm okays" have you forced yourself into
believing
Because you want to push that belief into everyone else?
Deep down inside that little girl that resides there just wants
everything to be that way
Girl the way you mask pain with that beautiful smile is
commendable
And the way you encourage others is so damn cute
You feed the souls of others even if that means yours will
go starving
You've always been one to put out more than you give
yourself
But do you take those words into consideration Queen?
Do you realize your amazing?
See I know you haven't always been the most confident
I know you never cared to be the most popular
I know about all the pain in your heart that still bothers you
I know how you love people even the ones you don't know
too well

And I know for the ones close to you,

you will go through hell

But when that cape comes off and it's just you in the room

You bleed

And you are left to heal your own wounds

Nobody ever comes to save the hero

and it's only but so much a bandaid can fix

but you know that already

I just want you to remember this

You are only HUMAN!

As real as you are, you are not perfect

I'll never understand how you try to heal the whole world

Even when your own heart is hurting

Drop those tears if you have to

Checkout from life and recharge that energy

Tackle those demons that tend to hinder you

Give some extra love to that inner you

Pray from sun up to sun down

Scream to the top of your lungs if it helps

As much as you'd love to save the world

Don't you ever forget to take care of yourself

Whoever's reading this, you need you too.

Heal (/hēl/):

To become sound or healthy again.

I remember having the biggest crush on this boy

when I was younger until one day he flat out called me

ugly. From watching him so often I already knew I wasn't

his type. He loved the popular girls. He liked the girls who

wore name brand everything and had straight hair or

weave. My mom forbid me to get any of that until I was in

high school. I was so hurt and confused. I thought I did

everything to make myself presentable. My hair was neatly

braided. My brand new sneakers weren't anything crazy but

they were clean. I was also a little more busty then girls my

age. I thought that was a plus when it came to attracting

guys. Sure I had a few acne scars and I wouldn't be me if it

wasn't a bruise or something on my legs. I was nothing like

the usual girls he went for but ugly was never a thought. I

always wondered but I never asked him why he thought

that. Believe it or not it bothered me for a long time after.

Years later I ran into him again. Of course I didn't speak but he had the nerve to yell my name loud as hell as if we were best friends who had lost touch. I ignored him and he made it his business to catch up to me and my friend. He started talking about how he always had a crush on me and was just afraid to tell me. He said he had a "rep to protect." I rolled my eyes so hard and then I just looked at him. He looked nothing like how he used to. He gained a tremendous amount of unflattering weight. His teeth were discolored, hair was matted and I had no clue what he was wearing. Only thing that seemed to stay the same was his pretty brown eyes. Once he was done talking his nonsense don't you know this man had the nerve to ask for my number? Yes y'all he tried me! Years ago he made me feel so inferior and here he was doing it again. So now that your rep was over and done you want to give the "ugly" girl a chance? I respectfully declined and kept walking with my friend. Next thing you know I heard him yell " Fuck you bitch!" I guess I wasn't the only one who turned him away lately. I was upset about him yet again calling me out of my name but I kept it cute. Well I did stick my tongue out and put my middle finger up but I didn't argue with him. As I sit here and reflect on that day I learned a few lessons from that horrible experience. The first was confidence is key! A man's preference in women does not take away from my beauty. Two was to never let anyone else's perception define me. Three was that the inside really does matter. No matter how good someone looks if they are a bad person it will turn me off every time. Truth is I was never ugly. He was.

SKIN

Fuck you if you hate me

You have no idea how long it took to love the skin I'm in

This melanin these high cheek bones and this gap that was

never corrected are just a few of the things I used to wish I

could hide

But now I confidently wear them with pride

I remember summer days when I didn't wanna go outside

because I didn't want to get too black from the sun

Or being in a group full of fair shaded women

being called "The pretty dark skin one"

Just being pretty would have sufficed

I guess that was their way of just trying to be nice

and its all right if you like what you like

And maybe you like your women light

I'm not everybody's cup of tea

Most people prefer coffee and I don't need no cream

I'm perfectly fine with being black

And I couldn't careless if you dread my locs

Or if the smell of the coconut oil

on my skin makes you cringe

Maybe you'd like me better if I put my bundles back in

Or if I was a few shades lighter than my chocolate skin

If I wore designer clothes instead of dashikis and shit

Would I be good enough for you then?

Maybe

But who the hell am I changing for?

I am unique, as rare as an antique, one of a kind

Baby they don't make them like me no more

I love me I won't change because you want me to

And really hate is just love miscommunicated

so in retrospect I really think you love me too

Don't ask me where I'm from

as if being from another place deems my appearance

acceptable

Dangling your standards of beauty over my head is

something I will no longer just let you do

Don't sugar coat my complexion in efforts

to make me feel better

I look in the mirror everyday and I like what I see

Yes I am black

I am proud to be black

I will always be black

And I am beautiful to me

Being hurt never made me want to go and hurt someone else. It made me wish the people who came before me could have loved them like I did. -Aliyah Michelle

I'm Sorry

On behalf of whoever hurt you like this

I sincerely give you the apology you never received

Every bit of pain they caused you is what you give to me

I know its not purposely but it's hurting me

I didn't break your heart but here I am willing to help you

put the pieces back together

Because I want you to be better

Trying to get you into the right motion

But sadly I think you've grown accustomed to being broken

I too have my own issues

But I stand strong for the both of us to stay a float

While other women have jumped ship

Here I am trying to find ways to steer the boat

Trying to get you in the right direction

Giving you all the love and affection I feel like you deserve

But what use is it for me to give you my all

When you look at me and all you can see is her?

I hate her

The cheaters, the liars, the ones who left you and the users

All the women in your past that have you scared

to plan a future

I know what they used to mean to you

I know they put you through it

But everything that you went through

understand I didn't do it

And I never will

The pain thats embedded in your heart

I hope you never feel with me

I know you took a big risk when you decided to deal with

me

and I'm always going to love you

as long as you keep it real with me

No matter what tries to break us down

I need to know that you're going to build with me

All that tough shit I see through

You're scared?

Nigga me too

But your heart is in my hands now

let me show you what a queen do

No gimmicks no lies

All I have is my loyalty and my word

All I wanna do is love you even if hurts

On behalf of whoever hurt you like this I'm sorry

You Like It

Maybe you like it

When my dimples peek through my cheeks

Laughing uncontrollably can barely even speak

As tears roll down my face I'm weak

And just to think moments before

I didn't even know what to say to you

Because no communication with me became ok to you

I ask, you lie

No matter how much I try to hide

I can't help the fact that I cry sometimes

There's no use in trying to keep my feelings to myself

Although I often feel like it's the best solution

But what's the use of showing you and telling you

I love you

If I can't even tell you what my heart is doing

Somewhere between those messages where you don't

respond, I wonder if I cross your mind

Or if you even care to know I'm fine

And if anything worth having is worth fighting for

It's only right that I wrap my hands, get my gloves

and put my sneakers on

But way too often I'm left in the ring alone

Waiting for you to put your dukes up

I guess it's gonna take a little longer for you to suit up

I hate to admit that you're my favorite bad habit

The stove my momma warned me not to touch

That sweet snack she told me not to eat so much

Because I'll get sick

I don't know what will come of this

Negativity feels my head even though I tell it not to

And I can't do you like you do me

simply because I'm not you

I ask, you lie

I swear I'm done and I lie too

I guess it will work itself out when it's time to

But I cry sometimes

Maybe you know this already

Maybe you like it

Mr.Pain

Allow me to reintroduce myself my name is PAIN

The only thing I've known for a while

The reason why I hesitate to smile

and I question everyone's gratitude

The reason why my vulnerability is limited and I always

get an attitude when someone gets too close

I've overdosed on sorrow

No need for the interventions or rehabs

I know the relationship we have is so unhealthy

Its sad to say the same thing that hurts me is what helps

It is my norm the only thing I look forward to feeling

because it lasts longer than anything else

You come and go as you please and it's so peaceful

when you leave

But I know in my heart you'll be back one day

You're the reason why I give love but won't allow

myself to receive it

The reason why when people tell me anything

I barely believe it

Because once everything is fine and I finally feel like

it's ok to shine

Your right back in my life in no time and in no time

All I feel is you

Face full of tears heart full of rage

thoughts all over the place

Praying about 3 or 4 times a day all I wanna do is be ok

But you're such a kill joy and you lurk waiting to rain on

my parade and I'm no better

No umbrella as I stand there while every drop falls on me

But thats over now, I deserve to smile

I wish you were a person so I can look you in your eyes and

tell you what I'm about to say

But somehow I know you'll get the message anyway

Mr.Pain, Don't you bring your ass back

Your bags have already been packed

Take everything you came with, leave your key on the

coffee table and do not leave your

toothbrush in my bathroom

Do not call my momma or any of my friends

You were bad for me from the start but

right here is where it ends

My life is my own and only God controls my destiny

You can lurk all you want but you no longer

get the best of me

You've nestled me in your arms for far too long

and strangely for a while that's where I felt like I belonged

I know that I can do better I know that I'm strong

And theres a light inside of me that can never be turned off

Mr. Pain you've been apart of me so long

but you've never fulfilled me

Today I reclaim my peace

I'm going to be happy if it kills me

God never removed anything out of my life
without replacing it with something better.
I'm currently preparing myself for better.
-Aliyah Michelle

The Cycle

You don't know how many times I had to say

Fuck you to somebody I really fucked with

How many "let's just be friends" I got stuck with

Let's be honest forget being modest

If we're going to do this right

I'm going to keep it a hundred

Even though I know what love is

I've loved too many times not to get it back the way I

wanted

I used to wear my heart on my sleeves as if they were

tattooed

Now here I am trying to repair the damages from the last

dude

How rude of you to ask me what my ex did

Then turn around and do the same shit too

Or ask me for things you weren't willing to give

You must've thought I was some kind of fool

I might have done that in the past

Let a few men play in my face

Tell me one thing then do another

Hoping to make the situation last

But a relationship takes two, there's me and there's you

I'm fighting for this bad

And you act like you can't see the problem

Boy it's simple do the math

It's you

You don't know how many times I had to say

Fuck you to somebody I really fucked with

How many "let's just be friends" I got stuck with

Damn. The cycle continues.

Never hold on to something you will have to heal from later. Let it go. If its someone let them go too. -Aliyah Michelle

Who You Are

Was it worth it?

That's what I ask myself as I sit here hurting

You showed me who you were and all I did was change the

frame because I wanted you to be picture perfect

But that isn't real and who wants that perfect love story

anyway right?

And as I sit here with this pen in my hand

Doing some soul searching and realizing who the fuck I am

I have a question for you

Who the fuck do you think you are?

Anything you wanted or needed

you had it from me

I would do almost anything that you asked of me

Everybody said that you were bad for me

Bad for me was an understatement

You were the worst

I neglected myself just to put you first

Y'all don't understand

If he was sick then I became his nurse

He needed clothes then he had my shirt

He needed money he could have my purse

What was mine was yours without question

But I can't say the same

And that's what got me going insane

Because I gave you everything any man would want

But when I needed things back then I'm asking too much

What the fuck?

All I've ever gotten was some unfulfilled promises

And too many "I'm Sorry's" to count on one hand

I gave my all and expected nothing because I wanted you to

be my man

You were everything but that

I just don't understand

Who the fuck do you think you are?

Dear Men,

We need peace too.

-Aliyah Michelle

Beautiful Lies

They ask how I'm doing

Who me? Im Okay

Just worked 16 hours to put food on my baby's plate

Because his good for nothing father couldn't

care less if he ate

Or where he's at or if he's safe

I'm sure somebody can relate

But besides that I'm good

My neighbor's son just lost his life to police

But after all I mean he was from the hood

And he had a bit of a record and he fit the description

"Black male walking from store minding his business"

How suspicious.

But I guess everything is great.

Made sure my coworker got home by eight

Because her husband will have a fit if she comes in a

minute late

Maybe he'll only hit her once this time or choke her against

the wall

or black her eye apologize and the next day forget it all

But other than that I'm cool

My little cousin dropped out of school

Because the three guys that raped her last year all got ruled

not guilty on all charges

How is that so?

She fought them her hardest, she screamed. She said no.

Now she's tricking and stripping five times a week six

maybe

Because now she's about to have one of her rapists' babies

No money for abortion and her parents

don't even claim her

They say it's her fault but how the hell

could they blame her?

But man I'm alright

Just prayed to God twice that the shelter would take this

child in so she can sleep at night

Both parents dead and foster parents don't treat her right

Two failed suicide attempts to escape this crazy life

So many women face these challenges

I don't live it but I've seen it

And I pray for the day they can say "I'm ok" and really

mean it

Abandonment, abuse, rape and suicide

Yet they keep on going trying to put their pasts aside

We don't always do what we want

but what we have to do as women

Trying to get a happily ever after from a painful beginning

So we stand up tall even though we're hurting inside

Put a smile on our faces and wipe the tears from our eyes

We're Fine

They only bring up your past

because they notice your growth.

Keep progressing.

-Aliyah Michelle

"Friend"

My mom said buy the time I get out of high school I'll be

able to count my friends on my hand

She was right

Yeah I used to swear that my circle was tight

I can call about twenty different girls when it was time for

me to fight

But ain't none of them around while I'm bettering my life

Because I changed

My mind different but yours isn't my fault

But I have to focus on my future if I want to make it far

You supposed to be my homie

you should still be on my team

But I can't do the shame shit now that I did at seventeen

That's some kid shit

And y'all act like y'all ain't never did shit

To make me sit back and have to second guess

why I'm in this friendship

But I've always been thorough

I was going through the trenches

But y'all bitches wanna fold

while I'm trying to build a business

And I don't mean to call them bitches

I still loved them this whole time

Still keeping secrets for the same chick who told mine

Once I love you I will always love you

And that fact always remains

But to get to where I'm going

I just can not stay the same

And can you blame me?

I got a few dollars, a dream and a baby

And I'll be damned if I let some little petty stuff phase me

I have a hand full of friends that's all I need in my life

Somebody tell my mom she was right

Missing Me

I didn't realize who I was anymore

All integrity had gone out of the door

Being so drunk in love, Better yet dumb in love

I forgot who I was living for

Watching every bit of my existence fade

Just to keep a smile on someone else's face

I nearly let myself slip away

As I learn to cut people out of my life

In order to keep my heart strings in tact

I notice the woman I used to be slowly coming back

There you are my love, I've missed you so much

Let's take care of those wounds and sores

I didn't realize who I was anymore

Stuck in a place full of misery

I have returned

You don't know how much I was missing me

Evolve (/ēˈvälv/):

To develop gradually, especially from a simple to a more complex form.

He cheated once again. He swore all he wanted was me. I didn't go looking for it she decided she wanted to "come to me as a woman." Where was all this integrity before? I'm posted everywhere on his social media and you still went and did what you did with him more than once. I was livid and I wasn't even going to let him know. I guess sitting at home watching marathons of crime shows paid off. Not even an hour went pass and when I tell y'all I dug up so much dirt on shorty y'all wouldn't believe me. I like legit knew where she went to high school, her birthday, where she lived, who her close friends were, where she worked and found out one of her favorite hangout spots. Not only did that have me questioning my own sanity but I started to be very careful about what I posted on social media. I promise that shit was too easy. I was ready to call my girlfriends up and we were going to track her down. How dare she hit me up gloating about what she did with my man? She had the nerve to have pictures too. I had so much anger built up towards her and then it was like I had an epiphany. Next thing you know I'm on the floor crying. Here I am putting together a whole plan to cause harm to this girl and I couldn't muster up not one consequence he was going to receive. I never thought to lay it all out on the table and see what he had to say for himself. I never thought about punching him dead in his mouth. I never thought to leave. He made a promise that he broke so many times and here he was breaking it again. The only person I should've been holding accountable was him.

I used to think people leaving my life was the

worst pain ever until I lost myself trying to get

them to stay. -Aliyah Michelle

Wasn't Me

I thought I could grow with you

Build a life, a family, be happy and grow old with you

They said you were a savage

And I still got a hold of you

Saw you had some baggage and my dumb ass just rolled it

through

But boy if I only knew how wrong I was

Fighting with you everyday

Arguing with you just because

And just because I didn't want to be single again

I convinced myself to stay

And you did the same thing again

Giving me the cold shoulder every time you're at home

When you fall asleep I'm going right through your phone

Fighting with every chick you decide to pursue

Thinking they were the issue but the problem was you

Yeah they knew about me and yeah it takes two

But the only one that owed me the loyalty was you

But I knew how you were so can I really blame you?

I guess it was my fault for really thinking I could change

you

No matter how good I was maybe I wasn't the one

Because a man will only change for the woman he wants

Maybe a future with me is something you couldn't see

As much as I don't want to admit it

The one for you wasn't me

Play Your Part

Do you not understand that you're the only person

who can fuck up what we got?

What does it matter how many people want your spot

Just play your position do you want it or not?

You're worried about a few comments

and what that man said

You would think every night I'm not laying in your bed

I could entertain these niggas but I curve them instead

Because for me half of them wouldn't do what you did

Yea he might cut a check

I heard he get a couple racks

But I watched you give me a hundred dollars

when that shit was your last

You put me on to game and taught me how to get a bag

You support me like no other thats some shit I never had

And sometimes you piss me off because you be acting like

my dad

But thats a blessing

I'm choosing you over them without question

So stop the questions

I'm not impressed with what a person got

If you got me then I got you

Either you with me or you not

I don't care much for words it's the action I believe in

As long as you show me that you're trying

I'm never leaving

I can compromise when it comes to a lot of

things.

Respect isn't one of them.

-Aliyah Michelle

Pay Attention

It's so funny how you can talk about me nagging and

bitching

But you don't even pay attention

I cooked our favorite food on Monday

But you wanted to go have wings with Neef

Tuesday I wanted to talk, watch a movie, lay up and rub

your feet

But you stayed out extra late came home and went straight

to sleep

Wednesday I put on your favorite night gown

lit some candles and put the kids to bed

Just for you to tell me

"Yo go get dressed" because Ant was coming over the crib

That night we argued

so Thursday you wasn't fucking with me

Friday we had a quickie

Saturday we both were busy

And Sunday I'm washing clothes and getting the kids ready

for school

While you do whatever you want to do

And your plans did not include me

Realistically I can't have all your time

And you can't have all mine

But I'll make sure the time we have is special

But the minute you make me feel like I'm begging for it

Im going to let you do whatever you want to do

Since that's what you'd rather do

Then we break up

And you see me and my new boo living it up

Then you're the one bitching talking about how I treat him

different

When in reality I'm doing the same exact shit

The only difference is he paid attention.

Once I love you I will always love you.

Even if it's from a distance.

-Aliyah Michelle

Petty Heart

I hope you never get the taste of a home cooked dinner

I hope all four of your tires go bald in the winter

I hope you never smile again

I hope the sun never rises where you lay

I hope you always have a bad day

I hope you never feel real love again

I hope you never get a good nights sleep

I hope every time you close your eyes you see me

I hope you have sex and say my name

I hope you feel me in your dreams

I hope you look for me in every single person that you meet

You took me for granted

And I know I'm at fault for being the hopeless romantic

And the girl that still believes in fairytales

But in this story I did not find my prince

The glass slipper did not fit

I wasn't awakened by your kiss

But by the reality of the fact that you did not want this

I hope you get the girl of your dreams sooner than later

And I hope she cheats on you with a basketball player

I hope she leaves without an explanation or a goodbye

And I hope every single night you cry

I hope every single night you cry

I hope every singe night you cry

I hate you

And I know right now I don't mean that for real

But I just wish I could make you feel how I feel

I hope these words pierce your heart like daggers and you

bleed nothing but regret

You've filled me with a hurt so bad I'm never going to

forget

But that's life

What happened between us just don't seem right

I don't mean to sound bitter but that's the way I felt

But maybe it was all in God's plan for me to make you a

better man for someone else

So let me stop speaking from my angry mind

And tell you how I'm feeling from my heart one last time

I love you

I want to see you live out every dream

I hope you succeed in every goal you wish to achieve

I hope your happy in every way

I hope your children are always ok

And I never want to see you have a bad day

We had our bad times but I hope it's the good ones you

carry with you

And I need you to know that I could never forget you

Our journey together has come to an end

I am not your enemy but I'm not quite your friend

I guess you can say it's complicated

But maybe one day I'll see you around

And not feel the anger that I feel right now

With time maybe I'll be able to greet you with a smile

I want to say thank you for everything that you've done

And thank you for being there for my son

Maybe after this awkward phase and when my heart finally

mends

I can really be able to call you my friend

But until this time comes take this lesson and live

And I hope one day my healing can begin

No matter what you go through in life never

stop being a good person. One day someone will

appreciate your pure heart and those who don't

receive your love anymore will wish they did.

-Aliyah Michelle

I can't speak for all women but I know that I want to be married one day. I want to be that wife that not only takes care of home, but can help to provide for the house hold. I want my husband and I to have a great relationship and an amazing friendship. With that being said I know there are some things about myself that need fixing first. I often attract people who need healing and I find myself neglecting my own wounds to cater to theirs. I know it isn't the right thing to do but that's just how I am. Next thing you know my insecurities surface. Then old scars that I know never properly healed are opened up once again. I don't want my future life partner to suffer because of anything in my past. Some people make the mistake of getting into a relationship while they are damaged because they've met the perfect person and don't want them to leave. I get it but I need y'all to know that shit is super selfish. You shouldn't rush to be the person they need you to be. Change takes a time and nobody is obligated to wait for you to reach your potential. If you aren't where you want to be emotionally, mentally and in some cases financially then it is best to stay single. If not you will damage anyone that comes your way. As much as it may hurt you both if you aren't one hundred percent ready let them go.

Wait

I was waiting for you

Please make me forget what the last man did

Because truth be told he got me fucked up in the head

It's so hard to trust, so hard to love, so hard to like

But you are exactly what I've waited for all of my life

You don't care that I prefer boots over heels

I love that you get money but I prefer my own bills

You like that I'm serious but I can still be silly

And even in sweats with my hair tied

You still tell me I'm pretty

I was waiting for you

I had no idea you would come this soon

I'm looking deep into your eyes

While you stare at my wounds

And I'll admit it

These days I'm thinking a little different

I want a relationship but I'm scared to be in it

When you least expect it that's when the blessings come

But I'm so afraid if I don't heal first that I will mess this up

I can't stop myself from pursuing you

But I don't want to ruin you

Have you paying for another mans mistakes

Next thing I know your wounded too

I know what needs to happen

but it's going to take more than a day

Might take months or maybe years

I can't expect for you to wait

I know how difficult I can be sometimes

I can't expect for you to stay

You're saying you can take it

I'm telling you I'm not ok

I don't want to lose you

But I'm damaged and I know that I'll abuse you

I'm always jumping to conclusions

And of course I assume too

You'll be my punching bag when I get mad

I barely be thinking but I react so fast

And when you don't answer your phone

I'll just think you were cheating

No matter what you say

I'll never believe you were sleeping

When we're in bed and I'm laying on your chest

You better not get no calls or answer any texts

You don't need no female friends, especially not your ex

Listen to the shit I'm saying

Can't you tell that I'm a mess?

You don't deserve that

I want to give you my best

A woman that's sure of her position

I don't want you settling for less

Let me get myself together

I'll understand if you run out of patience

I'll understand if you move on

But in my heart I hope your waiting

Without the experiences I've been through I wouldn't be able to create. If you ever made me happy I thank you. If you've ever caused me pain I thank you more. -Aliyah Michelle

My parents didn't know I could talk until I was almost two years old. Up until then I would only talk to one of my older sisters. I have always been shy and soft spoken. I feel like that partially contributed to some of the experiences I have gone through in my life. Having unhealthy relationships with men and friends are things that could have come to an abrupt halt if I had spoken up. I also felt like if I did say something they would leave. Fear of losing people will have you allowing individuals to stay in your life way longer that they deserve. I wanted people to be around so bad that I forgot how to just be happy by myself. Although I had eventually grown to love who I was, I lost myself trying to love others. I don't know how to give up on people I care about. It's kind of like the angel is on one shoulder and the devil is on the other. The angel is telling me to love harder. The angel says not to let go. The devil says forget them and leave them in the dust. After all that is exactly what they would do to me right? That angel always seemed to win because I found myself making excuses for the people who hurt me. I would find myself hitting that rewind button and giving them a clean slate. Most times they didn't even do anything to earn it. As much as I love imagining things I've come to the realization that there is no angel and devil on my shoulders. The only people constantly battling is the adult me and the naive little girl who lives inside. No one wants to be embarrassed. No one wants to be hurt. I would push whatever bad things they did to me to the back of my mind. Pretending to be oblivious to their antics, I would give them another chance. The adult me knows better than that. With time and experience I have gotten a little wiser. I've learned to silence that little girl when need be. It is nothing wrong with loving someone but if it isn't reciprocated they will drain you. Figure out exactly what you want and don't settle for less. Don't burn yourself out giving your all to someone who can't give you that same energy. Love is and always should be a two way street. Sadly, some people can't drive though. Whoever's reading this if you can relate to any experiences I've gone through I pray that you heal. I hope all the right people can feel all the love you desperately tried to give the wrong ones. I hope you are strong enough to demand more for your lives. I pray you are patient enough to wait for better. Some bad things may transpire but its all apart of the learning and growing process. I've never seen a rainbow without a little rain first. I give you permission to use my words as an umbrella. I speak nothing but great things into your lives. Thank you for reading. Sincerely, Aliyah.

Acknowledgements

God all I can say is you are absolutely amazing. I never know your plan but you have never failed me. I find myself being so emotional lately. I often cry tears of happiness because of what you've allowed to happen in my life. I am not perfect and I know you know that already. I just can't thank you enough for blessing me even when I don't deserve it. Thank you so much for this gift you have given me and for giving me the courage to finally share it with the world.

Amari there were so many times when you wanted to play and I told you to wait until I was done writing. So many times I know you'd rather be at the playground but you were stuck in the house while I memorized my poems. You have been so patient with me during this process. You motivate me to be better and to do better. Everything I am doing now is to secure our future. I want you to know you can do whatever you put your mind to. I will always support your dreams. I know I have visions of saving the world but I wouldn't be able to do anything without my little sidekick. You've given me so much purpose son. I thank God for you everyday. Mommy loves you stink.

At one point in my life I felt like I didn't need my parents. As I got older I realized that I need y'all more than I could ever imagine. I got my love for writing from my dad. Mom it's no doubt in my mind that my ambition comes from you. Dad passed away and you didn't miss a beat. You are the strongest and hardest working person I know. No matter what is going on around you you'll still find time to help others. I appreciate you for everything you do for Amari and I. Thank you for never judging me no matter how many times I fail. I love you mommy.

Sha thank you so much for being supportive. Thanks for being at every show and for reposting every poem. You have been my door person, the best auntie to Amari and anything I ask you to be even when you don't want to. To the only person I used to talk to, the one who potty trained me lol and the one who always has my back I just want to say thank you and I love you sis.

To Amari's God parents Chevelle and Mont we go way back. Y'all loved me and supported me when I went through almost every phase thus far. We grew up and went through so much together but we aren't going to get into all the details. Y'all have seen me at my best and have held me down at my worst. I am so blessed to have not one but two best friends in my life. Thanks so much for everything.

Steph I met you nine years ago and you've shown me nothing but loyalty. You tell me and anyone else what's on your mind even if no one wants to hear it. I can call you and talk to you for hours about any and everything. Neya at one point I feel like I was posted on your Instagram page more than you were. I never had to ask you reposted damn near everything with no problem. Even if you couldn't make my shows you are always one of the first people to promote them. Chrissy and Murder y'all were last to join the gang but y'all have been around for a lot. Thanks so much for coming out to the shows and even being apart of them when asked to be. Friends are an understatement y'all are truly apart of my family. I love you all so much. Thank you for being there for me.

Purple thank you so much for being in my corner

while I plan these events. Even if you can't be there physically you always support no matter what. You were the one making flyers and making sure I had everything I needed and you've never complained. I appreciate everything you have done and continue to do for me. If I've never told you just know you are amazing

Maui and Shakira y'all are seriously two people that I look up to. Whenever I felt myself procrastinating when I was supposed to be writing I would look at y'all and be like "Come on Lee you can do it." When I reached out to have y'all perform at my shows y'all agreed with no problem even though y'all didn't know me. When I hit y'all up for advice y'all give me complete honesty. Thanks so much for simply being who y'all are. We have so much on our plates being mothers and chasing goals. Watching you guys complete your books inspired me more than y'all know.

The both of you are so dope. You guys forever have my support.

Ken you took me to my very first open mic show. I was so nervous but I got up and went anyway. I did horrible that day but I kept going back. You took me to my first out of town show in Virginia. I thank you for allowing me to open up for a few of your comedy shows and for helping me plan my own events. You told me from the beginning that you wanted me to be great. With everything you had going on in your own life you still found a way to be there for me. We've been through a lot but I'd be lying if I said you haven't contributed greatly to where I am now. After all, you are the inspiration behind a few of these poems. I love you and always will. Thank you for everything.

Last but not least It's only right that I thank any and

everyone who has supported me since I've started. All the kind words you sent me have gotten me through the times when I felt like giving up. Thank you for all the comments, reposts and shares. If your name isn't in the acknowledgements please don't ever think you aren't important. There are lots of you who have been so great to me. This has been one of the hardest yet biggest goals I have ever achieved. Whenever I was in one of my moods it was the encouragement from all of you that kept me going. I seriously can't thank you all enough. I hope this book was everything you hoped for it to be or better. Whoever's reading this thank you so much.